Riding the Edge

A Life under the Reign of Bipolar

I0117222

Kevin Young

chipmunkapublishing
the mental health publisher

Published by
Chipmunkapublishing
PO Box 6872
Brentwood
Essex CM13 1ZT
United Kingdom

http://www.chipmunkapublishing.com

Chipmunkapublishing gratefully acknowledge the support of Arts Council England.

Author Biography

Kevin Young, born in 1963, has lived with bipolar disease all his life but was not diagnosed as such until 2009. How bipolar affected his life can be both sad and humorous. Learning to live with the disease without going over the edge is the hardest part.

Kevin Young

Chapter One
The Early Years

From the time I was about twelve years old, I knew I was different from the other kids but it wouldn't be until I was forty-six in 2009 that I would find out why. My emotions ran to the extremes. I could lose control over something and go into a rage, kicking or hitting whatever inanimate object was nearby, or I could obsess over a thing or person or go for hours or days full of energy over a project I happened to be doing at the time. Worse, my depressions were deadly, causing me to want to do anything it took to stop the pain.

I was born in 1963, at Cape Canaveral in Florida. My father was stationed there in the Air Force as a jet mechanic. After leaving the military, we moved to Wilmington, Ohio, which is where my parents were both from. My father, of Scottish and Welsh origin, had grown up in the country side and my mother (nee McAllister) had grown up the daughter of Clinton County's deputy sheriff.

When I was about six, we moved from Wilmington to Moraine, Ohio, then to Bellbrook and on to Appleblossom Place in Beavercreek, Ohio when I was eight. My parents moved to Beavercreek so they could both work at Kettering Memorial Hospital. It was in Beavercreek where I would start school and discover my life-long liking for girls of either Asian descent or white skin and long, black hair. When I was about eight or nine, we were watching television one evening and I saw a beautiful Asian woman on a program. I told my parents that one day I would marry someone like her.

Between hiking the woods behind our house in Beavercreek, yearly visits to Gatlinburg, Tennessee and the open forests around my various aunts, uncles and grandparents, I grew up with a love for the outdoors. As a young child, I was amazed by the flocks of hundreds of thousands of birds which went over in the spring and fall, taking hours sometimes to go over. Once, thousands of Monarch butterflies filled our trees in the Spring and took hours to leave. After the 1970's, when cities started spraying pesticides for mosquitoes, I noticed that these flocks of birds and butterflies dwindled year by year until no more Monarch clouds came and only a few hundred birds would make up the flocks that flew over.

It was also during the years in Beavercreek that I would develop a life-long appreciation for Euro cars. Father had a 1958 Jaguar and a Peugeot while mother also had a Peugeot. We would often go to the drive-in movies in the Jaguar and I would sit on the top on a blanket to enjoy Disney movies or classics like "It's a Mad, Mad, Mad, Mad World". Later in life, I would have several American muscle cars, but my favorite cars were the two Volvos I would later own. After my parents got rid of the Peugeots, they bought two Renaults. This was back in the day when Renault actually was a good car before their reputation became sullied in the 1980's.

I attended the local YMCA's summer camp for a couple of years where we would camp out at night, hike at John Brian State Park and learn how to sail at Cowan Lake outside of Wilmington Ohio. I will always cherish lake sounds. The sound of an oar against an oar lock, water breaking on the shore, herons calling from some tree... The sound of me crying from sunburns! And camp counselors also seemed happy to take us hiking through paths sided by nettles. Nettles do NOT feel good on bare skin.

I also played little league baseball. Or rather, I killed lots of grass by standing *wayyyyyyyy* out there, where I wouldn't do any harm. As a child, I had zero sports abilities. I was scrawny. I was a mutated mix between Opie and Howdy Doody. I hated both. Round white balls of all kinds have a tendency to seek me out in mid-flight and smack me upside the head while I am running between bases, or trying to hit them with a bat. Or I would be looking at the grass *wayyyyyyy* out there, where there was little chance that a long-fly ball would come towards me. I've always hated ball sports. Baseball, softball, tetherball, handball. Bowling, golf, football, tennis. I bowl what I really wish I could golf. I golf what I wish I could bowl. Bowling leagues love to have me join their team though because my handicap of 95 carries my team. There is something wrong with having a higher handicap than what you can bowl! In fact, the only ball sport I enjoy playing is croquet.

I attended Fairbrook Elementary from Kindergarten through fourth grade. It was in fourth grade that I met a Mexican girl who stole my heart for the first time. When in class, we talked rarely, but when recess came, we would head outside and start kissing. During my fourth grade year, I lost count of how many times a teacher would come and separate us and make her play on one side of the playground with her girlfriends while I had to play on the other side with my friends.

I also developed another passion in Beavercreek that would last my entire life; Bicycling. My parents gave me a boy's three-speed bike when I was about nine. Being an only child, I would often ride for hours through the plat of houses that connected to ours between Appleblossom and County Line Road. In later years I would purchase a 1992 Schwinn World twelve speed upon which I would put several thousand miles and see eleven accidents from racing too fast down steep hills and around curves.

While in Beavercreek, we raised rabbits. *Lots* of rabbits. The pen was about fifty feet long by fifty feet wide and at any given time we had around fifty or more rabbits. Father had half circle hutches of steel mesh turned on their sides and covered with plastic and these were covered with leaves from each year's autumnal tree dumps. The rabbits dug holes under these hutches to raise their families. We ran advertisements in the paper to sell them. People were forever coming to buy rabbits. I would spend hours sometimes, holding baby rabbits barely big enough to walk or just watching the babies hop around in the leaves. They were precious creatures at that age.

Up the road from us were an older couple whose backyard was full of flowers and vines. These two people cultivated flowers which would attract hummingbirds and butterflies and I saw my first hummingbirds there. They also had an abundance of butterfly and moth pupae hanging from foliage and they would have me come to their yard when it was time for these to hatch out. I saw my first Cecropia moths and Luna moths here.

In Beavercreek, I spent many nights outside in a homemade tent sleeping out under the stars. The local boys who were my friends there would often camp out with me here. There is something about sleeping out like that with the night sky so full of stars and waking up in the morning to the cold dew on the outside of the tent. It is an experience that is hard for others to relate to unless they have camped out themselves. Mockingbirds sang early in the morning and the dew was heavy on spider webs in the grass. Summers last forever when you are young and winters were made for reading many books and playing board games with my father. I also played heavily with tinker toys, lego, lincoln logs and GI Joe. Dad also taught me how to make igloos out of snow packed against 4x4 boards in the backyard so the igloo would last for days once the boards were removed.

From my earliest years, when I was first able to read, I started absorbing just about any book I could lay my hands on. Car books, dog books, horse books, westerns. Mystery stories, ghost stories, monster and science fiction. Every magazine we had I pored over, especially the Reader's Digest and Grit magazine. By the time I was into my late thirties, I had collected over three hundred books. I would later get rid of more than half of them due to outgrowing or being tired of reading the same ones. In fact, by the time I was 46, I had little interest in reading any more, not only due to having read everything I wanted to read, but because my bipolarity/ADHD wouldn't allow me to concentrate on anything for more than a few minutes at a time.

When I was ten, Father gave me a Crosman bb/pellet gun. From then on through the rest of my life, I never lost my love for rifles, and never developed an interest in handguns. I spent countless hours in our backyard with that rifle, waiting for starlings or sparrows to land so I could watch them disappear in the pull of my finger. Father taught me to love life though and about what birds never to hurt. Birds such as cardinals, blue jays, blue birds, finches and robins were off limits. Starlings and sparrows made a mess of our patio as they would arrive in flocks and cover it with their stuff. Later in life, when I was about forty, I lost any desire to shoot living creatures. To simply kill an animal for the enjoyment of it seemed morally wrong. I never had to kill to stay alive, so anything else seemed wrong.

Chapter Two
Troubled School Years

In Beavercreek also began something that would haunt me and almost destroy me later. I began being bullied. I was not a tall child, being small and thin. A tall blond haired kid at Fairbrook Elementary took it into his mind to destroy my world in fourth grade. He would find me in the plat riding my bike and throw rocks at me, or apples. Occasionally he would hit me in our yard or at Carroll High School where our bus transferred. There was no one to go to. I felt I would be taken as a wimp if I said anything about it. After fourth grade, my parents became Christians and moved me to Temple Christian School in Dayton, Ohio. To get there, I had to take a local bus, then a connecting bus at Carroll High School. The bully rode the local bus going to and from school.

In fifth grade I started attending church at Faith Baptist Church in Beavercreek. I soaked up the teaching from there but remember very little of my two years at Temple Christian. I remember the choir I sang in during 1976. We wore red, white and blue outfits and toured to different schools and churches, singing patriotic and Christian songs. I also realized during this time that adults were not perfect. The bullying I was going through was sometimes seen by adults who never once chose to do anything about it. In later years as a father, I stressed to my boys as they started their way through school to let me know if they were bullied. Knowing how I felt as a child, the hopelessness, rage and depression I went through, I feared what I would do to any child who bullied my children.

At Temple Christian, I also ran into the best and worst in adults. The pastor, Gerald Fleming, was a wonderful man. His whole family seemed genuine and happy to me. Later when I switched to Middletown Christian School in Middletown, Ohio, it would be the pastor's daughter who would drive me from Dayton to Middletown to go to school since my parents both worked at Kettering Hospital.

My grandfather, the deputy sheriff of Clinton County, also ran a small diner on the side of route 68 outside of Wilmington, Ohio. An event occurred there which would one day be immortalized into the movie, "Smokey and the Bandit" starring Burt Reynolds. Apparently an older man was inside the diner eating his food when some motorcyclists came in and started harassing him, doing stuff to his food and otherwise being butts. The man walked out of the diner and ran over their motorcycles with his eighteen wheeler! The story was also told in Reader's Digest by someone who lived in Wilmington.

Grandpa loved 'coon hunting. He had several bluetick hounds which he would use. He would take me with him on these forays into the hills of Adams and Highland counties in his El Camino which had a dog box in the back end. We would find some place far out in the countryside and he would set the dogs to run. We would sit for hours, talking in the cool of the night, waiting for the dogs to start braying somewhere, then off we would go, traipsing through the woods with Grandpa's 1941 Remington 511A Scoremaster .22 rifle. When

Grandpa later passed away, I would inherit this rifle from him.

In Fall, 1976, we moved to a house in the Franklin countryside so I could be close to the school I attended. Middletown, next to Franklin, was an interesting place to me. The first night we moved in, I saw flames jetting up into the sky in Middletown and questioned kids at school about it the next day. They told me the flames come from Armco Steel, Mfg Company. The flames were to vent off excess gasses and could be seen all night long. Our house was situated on three quarters of an acre with approximately one thousand acres of woods and fields behind it owned by various farmers and other landowners. Valleys, streams and ponds ran through these woods and were perfect for me. I would spend as much as nine hours at a time playing in the woods, hiking through trails, making my own trails, discovering the joys that this part of nature had to offer to me.

I also learned to use hiking, reading and bicycling to escape from the bullying. A couple of kids from Temple Christian had come to Middletown Christian the same year I did. They let other kids know the nickname I had accrued at Temple and literally overnight my name at MCS became "Howdy Doody" due to my short stature, freckly skin and lanky auburn hair. Certain boys within the school, about five of them, also took it upon themselves to make me the butt of nasty jokes and jostling or fighting. I can say honestly that I hated my five years spent at MCS. I made few friends. My bipolarity and ADHD were kicking in and I barely got through school with my grades. I was always being sent to the principal's office for swats when I felt like it was not my fault for acting the way I did. I made only three real friends at MCS, two of them boy-geniuses and one of them a girl several grades up from me, whose father owned a local equipment rental and sales company. Somehow, I think she saw through me to who I was underneath. I would go to her house where I became friends with her father and mother, and sit for quite some time talking with her father about this or that. Her father later gave me a Browning recurve composite bow.

One of the boys would be my best friend for fifteen years while the other would be a close friend for the last two years I was at MCS. Even his name was genius: Sherwin Wayne Dillard III. His genius level was probably out in the stratosphere range. He was of medium height, thin and lanky. He always wore dress pants, dress shirt, tie and a sweater like the one made famous by Mr. Rogers, but it was when we saw his first grades come out we realized we were not in his league! I think he made straight A's all through school. The other boy who I was best friends with for several years was also gifted in the intelligence area. His humor though was what endeared him to me!

Chapter Three
Friends

One day, while walking along with my Browning bow, I came over a hill to one of the ponds which were behind our house and saw John, (name changed to protect his reputation) one of the genius boys from school fishing in the pond. He saw me holding my bow, screamed, dropped his fishing pole and went running across the meadow to a farmhouse some distance away. I laughed for ten minutes over that one. I saw him at school the following Monday and told him it was me he had seen. We were immediate friends, sharing our common love of hiking, biking and music.

We started double dating together when we were about 18, learned to smoke cigarettes together and built incredible bicycles out of plumbing supplies. We would go to King's Island and pick up girls to spend the rest of the day riding rides with. We developed an easy camaraderie with each other and would often play practical jokes on each other. One day, I rode my bicycle over to his house since it was so close to ours. He was in the front yard using the riding mower to trim the yard. He did not see me arrive. I ducked over to the other side of the house where his apple orchard was. Getting off the bike, I started lofting apples over the house towards where I figured his mower was. At about the tenth apple, I heard the mower cut and then… *"Miiiiiiiiiisterrrrrrrr Young! Whyyyyyyy are you tormenting meeeeeee!?"*

Another time, in the winter, I drove over to see what he was doing. His Pontiac (mine until I traded it with him for a monster truck) was in the driveway but he did not come to the door. Now, I happened to have my .22 rifle in the car and started shooting a lot of the sparrows which were around. I killed a bunch, about fifteen. Deciding to be funny, I laid their bodies in a row on the hood of his Pontiac. Well... Later that afternoon, it snowed quite a bit. I was at home the next day when he called me. He said, "Mister Young, were you at my house yesterday?" I lied and said no. He said, "I was on my way to work at Kmart last night and the snow was blowing off the hood of the car when I started seeing these black lumps on my hood. I pulled over, got out and looked and it was a line of dead birds!" I laughed for probably twenty minutes over the phone at that one!

Still, another time, I came over on a nice summer's day because we were going out to run around that evening. I saw the back door was open but when I called he didn't answer. I figured he was in the basement taking a shower. Now, the outside water faucet was about twenty feet from where the shower was and when you turned the outside faucet slowly, it creaked loudly. I went to the faucet and slowly turned it and sure enough it creaked throughout the house. I did this slowly for a few seconds until I heard, faintly from somewhere inside the house, "*Hidddddddddeousnessssssss Mister Young!*"

John liked toys with large engines and would often spend too much money on them. He had a 1976 Ford F150 pickup truck which was nice to begin with. He took it further. He bought a 1968 Ford Mustang 390 engine and spent thirteen thousand dollars having it bored forty over, had a mid-size competition roller cam put in, competition lifter springs, had it acid dipped, blueprinted, painted and chromed then had THAT engine dropped in the truck. He then put large tires on the rear and small ones on the front along with a glass pack exhaust system. The day he got it back, I was in my bedroom with the window open, reading a book. I heard a roar coming down the road. Mother came to the door and said, "Kevin, your weird friend is here." I went outside and sure enough, he was coming up the hill, popping the clutch and rolling back down the hill, then roaring back up the hill to our house and popping the clutch again. The fourth time he did this, there was an enormous, "KABAM!" from underneath and his drive shaft fell down in the front and the truck started rolling backwards. Instantly, the look of pure glee on his face was replaced by horror and he yelled out the window, *"Mister Young! What was that hideous noise!!?"*

One day in the summer, John, his brother and I were sitting at the picnic table at his house just shooting the breeze after having done some target shooting with our rifles. John decided to run to McDonald's to get shakes. When he got back, he put all three down on the table and went in to wash his hands. His brother and I took our shakes and started drinking. Deciding to be funny once again, I took my .22 rifle and put a solid point bullet in and put the muzzle of the rifle right up against the bottom side of John's shake and fired the rifle.

It made a small hole on both sides and I wiped away the little bit of shake which leaked out and his brother and I just sat back and waited. Sure enough, John came out the door, picked up the shake and as soon as the pressure of his hand closed around the shake, milkshake spurted out both sides!

Hiking in the backwoods behind our house, I discovered many things that few people ever see. I found black snakes hanging from branches, sunning themselves (I brought one of these seven foot monsters back to the house, draped around my shoulders and just about gave mother a heart attack!), I found pellets from an owl where it had vomited out the pellets of what was left over from animals it had eaten. I saw hawks kill birds in mid air and saw a weasel kill a rabbit. I walked on a dam built by a muskrat (like a small beaver). I found hornets' nests which look like large pots hanging from a tree. Deer sign was always heavy as was coyote sign, although in all the years I tramped through those woods I would see neither animal.

In the mid-seventies, my parents and I attended several Christian concerts, introducing me to a whole genre of music I would forever love. Father had records by Ferrante and Teicher, who we also saw in concert, and introduced me to my love for classical music, but it was his Moody Blues' albums which I would truly cherish. They would later inspire me to write some of the poems I would pen in the late '70's and early '80's. Though rock music was non-sanctioned by MCS, we kids did dabble in it at home or in our cars. I became hooked on just about every kind of music there was at the time except country, which let's face it, really is not music anyhow!

In 1976 through 1977, I played on the school soccer team. Because I was small and scrawny and really did not like soccer very much, I rarely played. We traveled to other schools often though, and played some great games. Since school was only three miles from home, I would often ride my bike over during the summer practice sessions and ride back home afterwards. In 1977, Father gave me a ring he had, a black onyx with fake diamonds on it. I loved that ring because he had given it to me. I wore it always. Well one day during gym class, we played baseball on the soccer field. Afterwards we were walking back through the park next to the field and I was banging my bat on some cement blocks next to a few groundhog holes while holding my ball glove in the other hand. Suddenly, the air was filled with yellow-jackets. *I* was covered with yellow jackets! They started stinging me and I threw up both hands. The bat went one way, the glove went one way and the ring flew off and went another way.

I started running around in ever larger and larger concentric circles looking for the ring and screaming every few feet because I was getting stung. My classmates (fortunately only guys, no girls) were mostly all lying in the grass dying of laughter. Since then, I have sworn eternal enmity upon all bees and have gone out of my way to destroy them. I will even zap rubber bands at wasp nests. Several hornet nests have also had Armageddon visited upon them due to my wrath for bees.   Since then, yellow jackets have sought me out; laughing to themselves I am sure.

Chapter Four
Prose and Church

In eighth grade, my imagination started kicking in. I started having poetry come into my head and started composing it on paper on my portable typewriter. By my senior year, I had around twenty poems written, as well as the beginning of a full-length western and one short science fiction story. Louis L'Amour was my inspiration for writing the western, while countless sci-fi books from the library inspired me to write the short one. I also poured through Robert E. Howard's books as well as those by Zane Grey. By the end of my sophomore year in high school, I could type fifty-five words per minute and was the only boy in the typing class.

In 1976, just a month or two after starting at MCS, I asked Sherry Wheeler, one of my classmates, to come out in the hallway so I could talk with her. She came out and I asked her how I could be saved. She, being the class chaplain, told me shortly and briefly the Roman's road and there in the hallway I accepted Christ as my savior. From then on, I was at Grace Baptist Church (home of MCS) whenever the doors were open. I was there Sunday mornings and evenings, Wednesday evenings for mid-week service, and Saturday mornings for witnessing, where we men would go out to people's houses and talk to them about the Bible. I also became heavily involved in the youth department taught by Mike Mackey, as well as singing in the choir with some one hundred other people. The entire church usually had around two thousand people on Sunday mornings.

We guys in the youth department traveled around quite a bit and the entire youth department had many fun things planned and going on come Saturday nights, be it scavenger hunts over several cities for hidden envelopes with clues to the next envelope, or ice cream socials and sleepovers at the church. One year, we guys went to Dale Hollow Lake in Tennessee/Kentucky and spent two awesome days. We brought one raft with us but all the guys wanted to fish and I alone wanted to go boating, so I used the inflatable raft and spent hours on the water or across the lake hunting geodes on the shoreline.

On one such trip, we guys went to the Smokey Mountains to stay one night and come back. We went down early in the morning and hiked ten miles down into a deep valley, where we set up tents around a central campfire next to a roaring river. Nobody else was around except us. That night, Mike Mackey warned everybody not to yell "bear" as several of us had joked about it. We settled in for a good night's sleep. Sometime later, I woke to hear Mike Mackey Jr. yelling, "Bear! Bear!" and his dad saying, "Mike! What did I tell you about yelling 'bear'!?" Little Mike's voice came back from their tent and he said, "But dad! There *are* bears out there!" Sure enough, when we flashed our lights up the mountainside, four sets of eyes glowed out at us. They came right into the camp with us, snuffling around the fire and the trees. We had all of our food supplies roped up from overhead branches so the bears couldn't get to them and they left shortly thereafter. That was the highlight of the trip!

In 1978, the great blizzard hit. My German shepherd, Prince and I were out in the woods walking when it started. We stayed out there for three hours while the snow and winds blew heavily through, walking back to the house. Once the blizzard was over, we had drifts around our house upwards of fifteen feet high. I walked on top of the cars and only the antennae showed through the snow. I built an incredible snow cave in one drift and a snow couch inside of it. School was closed for two weeks, while some people had to stay at their work places for three or four days, existing off snack machines. Once the blizzard was over, I was able to go back into the woods and make a fortress inside some pine trees around which the snow had drifted. It was by far the most beautiful year of snow I had ever seen.

Chapter Five
Driving and Work

In 1979 I took driver's training through Franklin High's driving program taught by Bob Hoover. I received my license and started driving the 1978 Toyota Corolla wagon we had. I disliked that car. I was a guy full of guy urges to go fast and that car was powered by a rice burning rubber band. I learned the term, "neutral drop" and also found out that 1978 Toyotas do NOT go around corners fast. They also do not like being bottomed out over dips in the road at high speed, nor having neutral drops performed in them.

In 1980, I was friends with Dave Jackson, who attended Grace Baptist church but went to Franklin High School. His parents had a 1968 Oldsmobile Delta 98 with a 455 Rocket engine for sale for $250.00. My parents bought it for me. Oh. My. God. Guys at that age should not have a car that powerful. I could go through an entire set of rear tires at one burnout. Being in the country, I could fly through back roads on the way to school. Unfortunately, there were certain small peccadilloes about that car, such as air which liked to leak into the brake line. I was flying down the main country road one day towards school. I would have to come to a full stop to cross a main road (now where the new Middletown Hospital sits) then go up the other side to school. I was doing about ninety five. As I came towards the stop sign down the hill, I applied the brakes. Nothing happened. The brake pad went all the way to the floor! So not right! I went zooming through that intersection with both feet stomping the brake pedal, both arms fully extended on the steering wheel and my body straight out. I was literally standing on the brake pedal. If I had hit anyone, they would have been turned into jelly. As it was I flew through the intersection at around ninety and up the other side before the brakes started working again. I think I developed my first gray hairs that day!

My first job was working as a dishwasher for York Steakhouse, then Pizza Hut, then Godfather's Pizza, then Waldo Pepper's Pizza. Like almost every job I worked for though, I lost each one because I could not pay attention to what I was doing. I was on Ritalin during some of these years, but it did not help me. My emotions ran the gamut during these days. Losing a job would put me into terrible depressions where I would disappear into my bedroom and lose myself in reading or writing poetry.

My parents were both into selling Shaklee vitamins. Because they sold so much, they won a trip to the Shaklee convention in Estes' Park, Colorado and were loaned a new 1976 Cadillac d'Elegance to drive there. I had just gotten my driver's license so my parents allowed me to drive it much of the way. When we passed from Kansas into Colorado, it was as flat as a piece of paper. No mountains or hills to be seen anywhere. We drove about thirty miles and coming over a small rise, way off in the distance we could see a strange "cloud" formation. It was the mountains sticking up through the clouds. Driving towards Denver, I could see jets landing on the left side of the highway and taking off on the right side. I figured the road would turn somewhere along the way but it didn't. The highway went *under* the runway and the wings of the giant jets stuck out over the highway.

Going up into Estes, the air smelled so strongly of fresh pine trees, it seemed we could cut it with a knife. I had never seen such beauty before, having only the Smokey Mountains to compare it to. We stayed in the Holiday Inn Holidome and I made friends with several other people in their twenties who were staying for the same convention. One night, we had a Western Dress contest. I had a blue denim hat, white shirt with silver spangles, dark blue Jordache jeans and nice boots. After the contest, we five decided to walk up the road to the rodeo that was in town. We did not change out of our dress clothes and people were looking us over as we walked. When we got to the rodeo, we stood outside the gate watching the rodeo and then just climbed over the gate as if we belonged in the rodeo. Nobody stopped us because they probably thought we were part of it!

In my sophomore year, I was in Spanish class taught by Mrs. Moran. That year she and the agency, "Bearing Precious Seed" took us to Chihuahua in Mexico. We stayed at trailers in El Paso in the desert. In the morning small, yellow scorpions would be in the sink. The bazaar in Juarez, Mexico was amazing. They had everything for sale there at several dollars less than you would ever find in the states. At night, we showed Christian videos to the people of Chihuahua in the Spanish language.

By the end of my junior year at Middletown Christian, I had barely passed my courses, probably due mostly to my Attention Deficiency (hyperactivity). I had seventeen and a half credit hours, and needed twenty two to graduate, which meant I would really have to work my last year, plus I needed an algebra class in there and math was my worst subject. During the summer between eleventh and twelfth grade, I turned eighteen. I looked at Franklin Public High, which was only a couple of miles away, which only required eighteen credit hours to graduate. I was no dummy. I switched all my records to Franklin to attend twelfth grade there in the Fall with half a credit in algebra and all the other hours I had to be at the school in English courses. My parents were less than thrilled when I told them this news.

At Franklin, I already had several friends who went to church at Grace Baptist Church. I had hit my growth spurt and was six feet and starting to put on muscle from constant bicycling and swimming. As such, nobody bullied me at Franklin, but my emotions were still all over the place. It should have been an incredibly easy year for me, but I still failed algebra. I had to come back the following year for half a year to take the algebra class again and passed it with a C. The one great thing about Franklin was meeting Joe and John Campbell. Where my other friend John was my best friend when I was at my house, Joe Campbell and I became inseparable too. He played in the country band Cottonmouth along with his brothers John, Gene and Bill. Joe had a red 1968 Mustang fastback and we would often cruise for hours, drinking Pepsi Free or stay at his house, watching MTV which had just recently come out. It was 1982 through 1983 and these would be two of the best years of my life.

Chapter Six
Army

In January of 1983, with only a month left in my school year, I decided to enlist in the Army. Father had been in the Army then the Air Force and I had read much about the military through Soldier of Fortune magazine. I felt like it was the only way for me after graduating to do something with my life. I signed on for two years with me going to college afterwards on government money on the GI Bill. Five days after finishing my last class in February, I was on a bus to Fort Knox, Kentucky. I was psyched all the way there, thinking about how well I would do. We arrived at night and as soon as we got off the bus there were drill instructors yelling at the top of their lungs at us. It was at that exact moment, at about nine o'clock PM, that I realized I was a naïve kid who had no business being in the military!

It was hell to me, absolutely pure hell. I could never do anything right. When we were learning to load our M16 for the first time and slide it forward to engage the clip and then throw the switch, it should not make a sound except a slight click. Mine made a bang because it was in wrong. Fifty push-ups. Others learned quickly to never look a Drill Instructor (DI) in the face, never to smile, never to show emotion. I was full of emotion and always wanted to make friends with the DI's. Oh my God, what a mistake. I became "Ohio" instead of "Young". Basic training and AIT (Advanced Individual Training) were three months long. It felt like three years. I learned to shoot the M16, the M60 and the LAW (Light Anti-tank Weapon). I did well with the LAW and the M16. The M60 had too much kick and tended to rise on targets too much. The barracks were always cold, and the blankets were never thick enough, it seemed.

I was a souvenir kind of person and wanted one of the 7.76 bullets to take home, so one day on the range I picked one up off the ground and put it in my pocket. Someone saw me and reported it to the DI. Automatic Article 15. As the months progressed, I did well in running but came down with the sniffles, which magnified into sharp pain on both sides of my chest. Breathing became a true chore but I was still expected to run and do all the calisthenics. The base doctor for our company said I had a cold and gave me cough medicine. One night I pulled fire guard (where you walk around for one hour in the middle of the night and make sure nobody is stirring, then you wake up your relief). Due to the cough medicine, I made the mistake of sitting down once and fell asleep. Several hours later I was awakened by the Sergeant. Not good. Another Article 15. I was also vomiting blood at this time as the pains in my chest had gotten worse. The company doctor, when he heard this, told me I had pleurisy. The Army decided in its wisdom they did not want me and started proceedings to kick me out. In April, two weeks before I would have finished my full three months of basic and AIT, I was let go with a General Discharge.

I do have good memories though of being in the Army. One week while we were there, a company from Canada was staying up the hill in some vacant barracks. They were sharing the same chow hall we used. One night in April, it was warm and a heavy pea-fog rolled in. The next morning, looking out, we could see nothing as we got ready to go to breakfast. Suddenly, through the windows, we could hear one loan bagpipe start up. Then, a whole company of bagpipes joined in and we listened as they hauntingly made their way through the fog to the chow hall. When they stopped, you could hear clapping from every barrack within half a mile.

We also saw countless deer on the base. The base had a known population of some twenty-two thousand deer. I would be on guard duty at some small building in the fog, smoking my pipe with a fellow private and sometimes as many as fifteen or more deer would come out of the fog and watch us before straying off. I also drove an Armed Personnel Carrier (APC). This was like a tank but square in shape with a cupola on top where the APC commander would sit and where the 50 Cal rifle was attached.

Chapter Seven
Coming of Age and Bicycling

After coming out of the Army, a doctor told me that riding a bicycle would be a great way to get rid of the pleurisy. I started riding in earnest as it grew warmer. The spring and summer of 1983 began my nine year obsession with bicycling. I would ride almost everywhere. I had a car, a 1979 Chevy Kingswood Station Wagon, but I would very often use the bike to go places instead of using the Wagon. I got a job with Americana Amusement Park (LeSourdesville Lake) for the three summer months and would often ride my bike there instead of taking the car.

Americana started so much for me that was to go right for those three months and carry on into my life later. I had never dated during school as my ADHD kept anyone from being interested in me. I had such a low self esteem from too many failures that I hadn't asked anyone out except for one girl at Middletown Christian, and she told me she was already seeing someone. Americana was like the doors opening. I ran two rides during those three months - the showboat and the bumper cars. The showboat was a large, paddle-wheel driven boat, capable of holding thirty passengers. It had two Rolls Royce engines, each one controlled by a stick just like a tank or Armored Personnel Carrier. The engines were very powerful. If you pushed both sticks full forward, the boat would fly across the lake. Full back was reverse. One forward and one back would turn the boat in the direction of the one pulled back.

I became very good operating the boat, but after about a month something happened which caused me to be taken off the showboat and put on the bumper cars. I had a full load of passengers on a very windy day. I was backing up when my spotter who sat next to me suddenly noticed the paddle wheel was taking us close to the small boat rides which went through another section of the lake. I saw I was about to run into the barrier which separated the two rides so kicked the handles full forward. The paddle-wheel threw a HUGE wave up and over one of the small boats which had a grandmother and her grandson in it. THAT was my last day on the showboat!

While driving the showboat, girls would flirt with me. I started dating often during this time. Between the showboat and having this female attention, my self esteem started lifting up. I was moved to the bumper cars after the incident with the showboat. Bumper cars were housed under a large tent and controlled by a simple two button console. I sat on a wooden bench and watched people get in the cars, watched to see that they strapped themselves in and then I pushed the start button which would run the ride for five minutes. Another button was for stop just in case of emergency. Operating the ride was boring for me so I decided to liven it up. I brought in a squirt bottle in a brown bag so it would look like I had my lunch. The bottle would squirt about fifty feet in the air. There were pigeons always roosting in the upper parts of the tent. I would casually squirt a stream up in the air since most of the line of people had their back to me and the water would fall on them. They would look up, see the pigeons and... Well, the rest was me having a fun day!

During this time I was addicted to bicycling, sometimes going on one hundred mile rides in one day. Once, I ate a peanut butter sandwich in the morning and rode to Middletown Mall and back. On the way back, I saw five bikers on the side of the road getting water from a pump-handled well close to my house. I stopped in to see where they were riding and they told me they were twenty five miles into a one hundred mile ride. I rode with them the rest of the one hundred miles on only water and one sandwich.

Another time, I was at the foot of a large hill in Carlisle which I had been working myself up to for several weeks to ride. The hill was incredibly steep and long and every time I had tried riding up it before, I would hit the "wall" of that hill and have to get off the bike. This time I was determined to do it, and rode back about an eighth of a mile to get a good cruising speed. Suddenly, a girl in biking attire went flying past me on a beautiful bike headed towards the hill. I watched amusingly, not figuring she would get up it. But the impossible occurred and she flew up the hill. I could not let a girl better me on this hill so I took off too, standing up on the pedals to walk the bike up the hill with my feet firmly caged in. I made it up and saw she was headed for the second hill a half mile further on. I kept on going without stopping to rest. On the straight way between the two hills though, my muscles knotted up in my knees and I felt agony in them. I saw her make the top of the second hill and I went up it, stopped next to her because she was stopped watching me. I said, "Hi" and promptly vomited all over the ground! She was cool though and we rode quite a few miles together that day before parting.

One of my biking friends had six speeding tickets framed on his wall from bicycling. All six he had gotten from speeding through Centerville. The police would pull him over, take the bike in their cruiser and make him pay a fine to get his bike back. He was openly proud of this!

On another ride, a very eventful one, I was on a seventy five mile ride to Indiana and back with three other riders. We had a fifteen mile per hour tail wind pushing us out to the border. They went on at the border and I turned back to ride home. The fifteen mile wind was now a head wind and wore me out. When I finally made the top of the hill which was up the road from my parents' house, I laid my arms down on the handlebars and rested as I coasted down the hill. Somewhere between the top of the hill and my parents' house, I fell asleep and woke up in the ditch with a mangled bike and bloody head!

Chapter Eight
Middletown Area Rod Association

After Americana, I worked at a few odd jobs until 1985 when I became the office manager for P&M Industries in Middletown and Cincinnati. My manager would put ads in the paper needing people and I would weed them out when they called back depending on what kind of phone voice they had. I would bring them in for interviews, then hire and train them to call people on lists and try to get people in for timeshares at local parks and give them free prizes. It was during this time that I bought the car which would initiate me into the world of hot rodding, a 1966 Chevy Impala. My friend John and I painted it blue with red racing stripes on the hood.

I started hanging around the Burger King in Middletown on Briel Blvd. By and by, I collected a group of about forty other rodders. We became a major presence at Burger King for the next two years. We would sit in the parking lot with our hoods open and people would come through and look at our cars and engines. Some of the group was truly different. We had one guy we called Stubbs because he was missing part of a finger. His father ran a mortuary in Post Town. Stubbs would come down the road in his 1978 Cadillac Hearse, with two or more Ninja motorcycles preceding him. On the back of his hearse was painted, "Heavenly Bodies" and the inside of the hearse was wall to wall white carpeting with a drum set and amplifier for his guitar. Stubbs also wore a full length leather coat and a Captain's hat with sunglasses on.

We had cars from all through the fifties, sixties and seventies. We would race each other or other rods on the Southern end of Briel Blvd then meet back at Burger King, White Castle, or the Mall parking lot if it was really late. Often we were in one of these places until daylight the next day on the weekends. We took over Smith Park in North Middletown and people would again cruise around so they could look at our cars.

A small group of us were very tight. It was inevitable that some of us would play jokes. Jimmy Keller, one of the Pontiac drivers, was a high strung individual. His car wouldn't lock right so he left the doors unlocked when he worked at the pizza joint near Smith Park. One night, I left my car at White Castle uptown and three of us jumped into one of the other guys' cars and drove to the pizza joint to see him when he got off. On the way there, we concocted a practical joke to play on poor Keller.

When we arrived at the pizza parlor, I got into Jimmy's back seat and lay down and the guys went in all excited, telling Jimmy that Kragan had had a wreck (Kragan was the name of my car so everyone called me this). They told Jimmy I was in a serious condition at Middletown Hospital and that I wanted my best friends around me but that they needed to stop at my car and get some stuff out (music tapes). Jimmy explained the situation to his manager and rushed to the car, unaware I was in his car already, in the back seat. He rushed uptown to White Castle, talking to himself all the way because he was so worried and stressed out.

As we came around the corner of Briel Blvd to turn into White Castle, he saw my car sitting there untouched and went, "*What*?" At that moment, I rose up out of his back seat and grabbed him by the shoulders and yelled. Jimmy almost had a heart attack!

Yet another time, Devo (Doug Johnson's handle because he looked like one of the guys from Devo) and some others were parked at White Castle along with myself. We were sitting on the hoods, smoking cigarettes and just talking while eating White Castle burgers. I got in Devo's Oldsmobile and put his emergency brake on, then got back out. Later, he left and we all watched his car literally lurching down the road and chirping the rear tires every few feet. But... my payback was coming.

A couple of nights later, I was in Burger King eating with some of the other guys and girls and Jimmy came running in telling me that Devo had wrecked his car because someone had put the emergency brake on. Jimmy told me Devo was out in his car. I went running out and sure enough, Devo was sitting in the passenger side of Jimmy's Pontiac with heavy bandaging on his head, right shoulder and right arm. He looked terrible. I got in the car and apologized and told him it had been me that had applied the emergency brake. I told him I would give him my car. At this point, he started making these strange noises, then couldn't control himself and started laughing out loud in earnest. He then pulled off the fake bandages so I could see there was nothing wrong with him. Dirty rat!

I was home one day at my parents' house and the phone rang. A girl was on the other end asking for Mike. I explained she had the wrong number. She asked what number she had dialed. I told her and she told me our number was one number off from Wendy's where her girlfriend's boyfriend worked. Her name was Lisa and we ended up talking for two hours, agreeing to meet later in the week. I drove over and met her in Carlisle, Ohio. We liked each other immediately. For several months afterwards, we would be dating. I met her friend, Trish and am afraid I was attracted to her. Trish looked like Demi Moore before anyone knew who Demi Moore was. When Lisa and I broke up, Trish and I started dating.

I left my job at P&M Industries because the money I was making did not pay for the gasoline in my Impala. Between driving to Cincy and hot rodding, I did not have much extra spending money left and my parents wanted me to grow up and move out. It was during this time that I started going to church on Sunday mornings, only to leave while the opening prayer was being said because I wanted to hot rod with my friends. I had stopped going to church completely except for Sunday mornings. One of those Sundays, it was as if God were there telling me, "you can stay in church where I will do something with you or you can go hot rodding and lose it all." I literally knew I was at a crossroads at that moment but I continued and walked out. From then on, I did not go back to church throughout 1985 or 1986.

Chapter Nine
Signs of the End

I took a job at Southwestern College of Business in Tri-County, Ohio and started saving up to get an apartment. I was burning the candle at both ends though, working all day then staying out late with my friends. My bipolar and ADHD started causing me problems at work, in that not only could I not pay attention but I was going through tremendous depression because I was not enrolling students the way I should have been. I was chain smoking three and a half packs of cigarettes daily and was on a downward spiral. The depression only made me less effective at work and I smoked more to stave off the stress. We had a quota of students we were supposed to enroll and I could not meet my quota.

Mother, seeing my life going downhill, took me to Dayton to talk to a pastor. He advised me to park my car and join a program called "New Life Ministry" at a place called the Dayton Gospel Mission. Instantly, I had a mental image of the kind of mission like the one in Chicago with winos and homeless people and I thought to myself, "Yeah, right, I am going to leave my popular life, park my car and live in a mission on some sort of program". I was to learn that God was giving me a last chance and again I failed to listen.

In July, shortly before my birthday and shortly before I had promised my parents I would move out, I lost my job with SCB. Deeply depressed, I left a note on my pillow at my parents' house telling them that I was leaving and that I was sorry. I met with my friends at White Castle and told them I was running away. They did not understand but I pursued the action and at two in the morning, left for Tennessee. I had my sixteen foot kayak on top of the Impala and my bicycle in the trunk along with my clothes neatly folded up. I intended on going to Dale Hollow Resort where I had once gone with Grace Baptist Church and row myself out to one of the islands and starve to death.

Arriving at the lake, I parked and unloaded my kayak and camping gear. I kayaked out to the far side to a deserted beach. Dale Hollow is a very long lake with most of it being very quiet. I set up my tent and sleeping gear and settled down with my cigarettes, bent on starving myself. I stayed for all of two days. The depression broke and I paddled back to the other side and called my parents, letting them know where I was and that I was OK. Mother was so stressed over the note, afraid of what I might have done.

Going back to Ohio (it was July, 1986), I started living in my car. I had nowhere to go. I would live in my car from then until late December. In October, the engine blew, probably due to not changing the oil. Jimmy pushed my car with his out to a vacant house in the countryside and I lived there, in my car. My friends brought me food, be it pizza, fried chicken or takeout. I had bottles of water in the car. I would ride my bike to the local truck stop to wash my face and hair in their sinks. When the cold weather settled in, I would pour a little bit of cologne in the metal pullout ashtray and light it. The heat from that would fill the car. Finally, it got so cold that in the mornings I would wake up and there would be ice caked on the inside of the windows from condensation from my breath. On December fourteenth, I prayed to God and told him that He had two weeks and if He didn't do something, I would walk out in the woods and let myself freeze to death on the ground. I was at the end of it all.

A week later, my mother found me in the car. She told me to get ready at their house and she would take me to the Gospel Mission to talk to the director there. I agreed. We drove to Dayton and I talked with Ken Clarkston for a while. It was agreed that in a week's time, I would come to live at the Mission. Two weeks exactly to the day that I had prayed to God to do something, He did. I told my parents to sell the car and I left the boat and bike at my parents and moved into the Mission.

Chapter Ten
The Mission Years and Sinclair

The Mission was huge. It was actually several buildings with a main building and two houses. The main building had a large chapel and living quarters below along with a large kitchen and a well-stocked library. There were three other young men living there, all three from Puerto Rico. They had come to America to study under the martial arts instructor Stephen Hayes. After studying under him, they had no money to go back to Puerto Rico. Our part at the Mission was to help in the day to day chores of the Mission such as fixing meals for the overnight men who stayed, cleaning the Mission, unloading supplies from the various trucks that came in and then taking Bible classes at the Mission taught by the director.

Ken Clarkston had given up a lucrative electronics company to take over the Mission. He was studied in the Bible as only a pastor could be and taught us all that he could, including much Greek and Hebrew. We also attended Emmanuel Baptist Church on Sundays with Ken and his family. The Mission served meals every day with a lunch and supper being served on Tuesday and Thursday. At a certain time of the evening, we would start taking in homeless men who would line up outside the building. We would allow them to take showers and then go to bed. In the morning, we would fix them breakfast and usher them from the building. Before meals, people sat in the chapel and listened to Ken preach, or a guest preacher would come in.

We four guys stayed in the Mission itself and each of us had our own room. We ate like kings though because the best food was donated to the Mission. The local hospitals would donate their leftover foods along with that coming from the doctors' cafeterias. Honestly, the Mission was very unlike the way I had imagined it. Coming in at Christmas time was hard because there was so much going on at the Mission in the way of programs for the homeless and local community that we had to be a part of.

As I became part of the Mission, I became familiar with who worked there and their lives outside the Mission. The secretary, Carol Koblentz and I talked one day and found out that she had been married to John Wheeler in Franklin, Ohio and had children with him, been divorced from him and was remarried. John Wheeler remarried and had other children from this marriage, one of them being Sherrie Wheeler, the same girl who had led me to Christ all those years before in 1976.

Carol was also a practical joker. She found out from me that the wages I had made in 1986 hadn't been reported to the IRS because I was living in my car. One day she gave me a letter addressed to me from the IRS telling me that I was being charged with not reporting my taxes and I owed back taxes and possible imprisonment. I panicked big time, until one of the guys pointed out the signature, "U. R. Lame". Very funny, Carol.

In Spring of 1987, once things had quieted down from the Christmas season and we each had become comfortable in our positions at the Mission, Ken announced that he wanted all four of us to go to college at Sinclair Community College in Dayton. Living at the Mission would allow us to go for free as we would be eligible for full government grants. We each filled out paperwork at the college and were scheduled to start in the fall of 1987. One of the boys decided not to go, which just left the three of us. I chose Liberal Arts major with dual minors of English and computer science. I already was comfortable using computers from bootleg time at Miami University in Middletown hacking their Apple IIc's. I also was heavy into the bicycling bulletin boards on the Mission's computers.

Just because I was at the Mission did not make my bipolar problems go away. Some days, I gave up on myself and it was only the fact that Ken and his staff did not also give up on me that I stayed. Other days I was so manic and angry that I got into trouble for my rage problems. I would kick things out of sheer anger when nobody was around or if something unplanned happened in my daily schedule. I did not know why I was the way I was, only that I was a trouble maker and could not control my emotions.

Spring turned into summer at the Mission. We guys had fun with each other outside, playing ball sports and frisbie. We were very busy at the Mission every day but usually had a couple of hours to ourselves. I would read alot but we also had exams we took on the Bible. When school started, Ken or one of the staff would drive us to Sinclair and then pick us up at the end of the day.

I found myself at Sinclair. Like hot rodding, I was able to pour my passions and obsessions (bipolar causes obsessional behavior) into school work. I excelled at every class I took. I was fully loaded down but it did not seem hard. Ken gave us extra study time so we could cope with our classes at Sinclair along with Bible classes and chores at the Mission. I felt enlivened and energized when I was at Sinclair.

It still did not keep me from playing practical jokes though. In one computer class at Sinclair, when everyone was gone, I went around to each computer in the class and set the auto alarm to pop up during a class the next day which would say, "This computer infected with Trojan worm. Contact your administrator immediately." I heard about that one through talk around the school after it went off!

I was invited to join the Campus Bible Fellowship and became Vice President. There was a gay group at the school called "Open Doors". I decided to have some fun with them. Sinclair is three stories tall with the center of each area being open, so you could stand in the third floor section of classes and look down on the second and first floor classrooms. I printed out on continuous form paper a thirty foot banner which said, "SAY NO TO OPEN DOORS, KEEP GAYS OUT OF SINCLAIR". Since we arrive early in the morning, when nobody was around, I hung two of these banners over the ledge so they would hang all the way down to the first floor. Again, I heard that security was mad to find out who had done this.

Time flew by at the Mission. I stayed friends with two of my main contacts from my hot-rodding days. They could not understand why I would be in a Mission, much less my dedication, but we were friends. That friendship dropped off by and by as it became hard to maintain friendships like that over the fifteen mile distance. In 1989, two of the Puerto Rican guys and I moved over into one of the homes, called an "Honor Home". It was a brick town house that had been completely redone. We each had our own room again and it gave us room to do our studying.

The government covered my classes one hundred percent as well as books. I always had some money left over each quarter too. In 1991, I paid two hundred and fifty dollars to buy a 1992 Schwinn World twelve speed and then paid to have modifications done on it to make it lighter and faster. I started biking to school, tearing through the downtown streets of Dayton like a maniac. I used one of the above ground bike lockers to keep my bike in and kept it stocked with cases of diet coke. I also started biking extensively in my free time, all around Dayton, to Franklin and surrounding areas of Dayton into the countryside. I even had a bike cop pull me over downtown one day asking me to keep my bike in one lane as I was zooming in and out of traffic.

It was in 1990 that a new staff member came on board. April (named changed to protect family) was Chinese and a chef. She was 46 at the time and I was 26. Now, by 1990, we guys were allowed to date as long as the girl was Christian and known to the Mission staff. This usually meant Cedarville girls who would come to the Mission to help with chores. I did not date anyone, although my two friends at the house were dating. I did date one girl from Bob Jones University for a while but we really did not fit each other's "type". We guys also in no way could date staff.

April's ex husband had just recently died and she had grown children already. She was the child of one of Chaing Kai-Shek's officers from when the Communists took over China and ousted Kai-Shek. She even showed me a picture of herself as a young girl holding her father's hand and being welcomed onto a ship by the U.S. President in 1948. Her father was then assassinated a short time later. Somehow, April and I recognized kindred spirits in each other immediately. April knew I loved bicycling and asked if I knew where Lincoln Park (home of Fraze Pavilion) was. I told her yes and she asked if I would like to meet there and walk sometime. I said yes.

One Saturday afternoon, we arranged to meet at the park after she finished cooking for the next days' meal and I finished my chores. We met and walked around the park after I bicycled up to the park. Then, there was only a small building there. The Fraze had not been built yet and few people visited the park. We sat down together next to the building, which was where they kept their chairs for small events. April took my hand and looked at me and I was gone at that point. From then on, we clandestinely had a two year relationship until after I left the Mission. Sometimes, one or the other of us would go to that small building and leave small messages in pencil on the window sill, written very small so nobody else would see it except for us. It was our romantic meeting spot.

April had a condominium in Centerville. I could bicycle to it in one hour. She gave me a key as well as an extra key to her car, an Audi. We started meeting closer to the Mission where I would put my bike in her trunk and then I would drive us to her condo. She would cook meals for me at her place, or we would go to the lake at Houston Woods, Ohio. We lived with the stress, though, of having to pretend nothing was going on for two years while we were at the Mission.

We went many places together. One time, with both of us dressed in white shorts and white polo shirts and white shoes, I drove us to the woods behind my parents' house and drove the Audi back a lane into a field where I could hear someone combining corn. I parked her Audi next to the corn field and we carried a picnic basket and wine back into the edge of the woods. Because it was very dry, the combine was throwing up a lot of dust, so when I heard him coming near the Audi, I went to the car, holding my wine glass in one hand and keys in the other, to put up her windows. The guy in the combine was just sitting there, idling his engine, and the guy was looking at me and the Audi like I had just fallen from Mars. That was a funny one!

School, meanwhile, was going as well as it could. Where I had failed my way through high school, I was on every list for college. I was on the President's list almost every quarter along with the Dean's list. I was in Honor's English and Honor's Psychology. When I gave speeches in Honor's

English, the President of the college came by once to listen in. There were only twelve people out of eleven thousand students who were picked to be in the Mid-East Honor's Association and represent the college in the Honor's regionals and I was one of them. Out of us twelve, two of us, myself and a girl, were selected to go to Las Vegas to represent the college at the National Honor's convention. The girl got it and not me because she had joined Phi Theta Kappa and I did not have time to join it along with my other work at the Mission.

I was taking Economics. I only had to take Econ one and two but I also took three because of who taught it. His name was John Burke and out of two colleges I attended and two high schools, he was absolutely the best professor I ever had. He was an amazing man. He was about sixty years old and wore jeans and a flannel shirt unbuttoned down two buttons from the top. Professors at Sinclair were *supposed* to wear dress outfits and ties for the men. He had been there so long he could get away with it due to his tenure.

We would be in class and he would always come in ten minutes late with a McDonald's straw between his teeth and the top of a coffee cup on the straw. He would come in, put his coffee cup down along with the straw and say in a gravelly voice, "Kids, you know how much your government is going to do for you today?" Then he would hold up his right hand in the OK or "zero" position, put his left hand under the right elbow to accentuate the motion and move his right hand around vigorously to show "zero". Then he would tell us how today he was going to teach us how to take care of ourselves in the economy instead of relying on a crooked government.

He was severely right wing like me and fervently hated the liberals and democrats. When the first Bush was up for election, I brought in huge continuous form posters that said, "John Burk for President. Kill the Liberals and hang the Democrats!" Nobody saw me hang the posters up because I rode in early one morning and hung them up with duct tape. When I came to class later in the afternoon, people were standing around looking at the posters and talking openly about them as everybody knew what Mr. Burke was like and everyone loved him. We went to class and sat down. He came in and one of the kids said, "Mr. Burke, are you going to run for President!?" The class laughed. He put down his coffee and straw. Then, he looked right at me and said, "Kids, let me tell you two things that are sad. One is that someone would hang those posters up in the first place and two is that someone would know me that well!"

My last quarter at Sinclair I dropped back in GPA a bit. I had to take college algebra and again, I had a tutor but I only got a C in the class. I also took shorthand and received a D because I hated the class so I ended up auditing it. With ADHD, I could not make myself take the time needed at the house to write those symbols out over and over until I remembered them.

I took a piano class which was fun and a voice class which was also fun. All in all at graduation, I had one hundred and twenty credit hours with two minors. April was also taking some classes at Sinclair now after hours at the Mission and she and I openly walked together, knowing I would be leaving the Mission soon.

In January, 1992, The Mission gave me a 1976 Pontiac which had been donated. The car was in mint condition. In March, April told me that two of her Chinese friends who were married owned a computer business in Kettering and were interested in me. I was interviewed and got the position. I started in April of that year, driving the Pontiac back and forth. In June staff at the Mission helped me move out of the Mission into an apartment in Kettering not far from work. I learned how to build systems, and upgrade and install software. Then it all went bad. I was fired in July. They told me it was because I did not do my job well. April told me that I was fired because the wife was jealous of April dating a white guy half her age.

About this time, I drove to Grace Baptist Church in Middletown for the first time since 1984 to visit on a Sunday. I dressed the way I was used to which were black pants, white dress shirt, red tie and a black dress jacket. I also had my large red Bible in its red leather cover. I sat down at the front of one pew and waited for services to begin. There were about 2000 plus people there that day. An usher came over and gave me a card to fill out. It asked for my name and the church I was coming from. I filled out my name and Immanuel Baptist as my church. The usher asked if I would mind giving the offertory prayer. I had no reason to say no, so I agreed. After some singing, the pastor there stood up and said, "Visiting with us tonight is *PASTOR* Kevin Young with Immanuel Baptist Church in

Dayton!" I couldn't correct him in front of all those people so I quietly gave the offertory prayer and sat back down. Ken at the mission jokingly told me I would probably burn for that!

Chapter Eleven
On My Own and Mai

In 1984, I had taken a cooking course in Cincy for six months. I fell back on this and applied at Dorothy Lane Market. I was hired at the Washington Square store as assistant chef. The pay was considerably less than what I was making at United Computer Resources, but it was enough for me to live on. It was at this time that April and I had problems. Between losing the job and my occasional outbreaks of anger over relatively small things, we broke up in July of 1992. I was devastated. It felt like an emotional punch to the stomach. I heard she married again but was only married for a short while when she passed away due to lung complications.

I started my friendship back up with John again. He loved my Pontiac. He still had his massive truck and asked if I would like to trade. I thought he was kidding. I even asked him if he was kidding. He wanted the Pontiac so he could use the engine in another Pontiac he had. From then on, I had the monster truck. I really should not have traded though, because the Pontiac got good gas mileage and the truck...well, didn't get any mileage at all! Fortunately, DLM was not too far from where I lived.

After being in such a relationship with April, I could no longer be alone. I remembered seeing a cute Vietnamese girl at Sinclair several times walking around and drove to the school and staked out the areas where I had seen her before. Sure enough, I ran into her one day. I introduced myself and asked her if it would be OK if I called her sometime. She said her name was Hoa Nguyen and asked if she could just have my number instead. I gave it to her. In October, she called me, asking if I remembered her. I said yes. She asked if I would like to meet her sister, Mai instead. I thought this odd, but said yes.

Mai is Hoa's older sister. Mai was not in college and did not speak English. Hoa wanted me to teach Mai how to speak English because of my background at Sinclair. We met and I was taken with how pretty and cute Mai was. But I kept it professional. We met three times at Burkhardt library for teaching. I would generally spend about one hour each time with a dictionary and notebook paper. I would show her words for daily things she might run across and teach them to her and she would ask me about other words. She also used a Vietnamese to English dictionary to show me words and ask me their meaning.

In January of 1993, she asked me if I could take her to a movie. I said yes and we drove to a local cinema. Only three movies were showing at the time; "Beauty and the Beast," which she had already seen and I had no interest in, "Scent of a Woman" and a movie called "The Lover", which was filmed in Saigon, Vietnam. Mai said she wanted to see that one. I thought, Oh great, what kind of movie is this with a title like that? So we went in. Oh my gosh! I sat there in the seat petrified. It was an extremely rated R movie about a young 14 year old French girl living in Colonial Saigon who has a much older Chinese lover. I wondered what Mai must be thinking about the love scenes. She said nothing however, and I dropped her back at the library where her car was.

Mai and I started going out at this point through the rest of January and February on dates. Her English improved greatly as the days went by. By the day before Valentine's Day, 1993, I knew what I wanted. At ten minutes to midnight that night, I asked her to marry me and she said yes. As the months went by and she got to know me, she knew that I could not stay at Dorothy Lane Market making the pay I was. She told me she saw potential in me. Her oldest sister lived in Tennessee with an American husband who had been a GS15 in Vietnam. They wanted to get to know me and there were jobs open at the Johnson Controls factory there, making Ford parts.

Mai lived in Riverside, Ohio, just east of Dayton and west of Beavercreek. She lived in a large two story bi-level brick house along with four sisters, two brothers and their mother and a niece and nephew. The entire family had come to Vietnam in 1990 and most of them worked for Morning Pride Manufacturing, in Dayton, Ohio, as seamstresses. Mai was three years older than I but looked like she was in her late teens.

In January, 1994, loading up my truck with all my belongings (I had a pickup shell to put on the back too) along with my bike and boat, I said goodbye to Mai and moved to Lexington, Tennessee. I was so lonely and depressed being away from Mai but it was for a greater good. Khuyen and Harold Segerson are Mai's sister and brother in law. They own a number of buildings in

Lexington, including some apartments downtown. I moved into one of these apartments and paid two hundred and fifty a month for one of them while working eight to twelve hour shifts at Johnson Controls.

Chapter Twelve
Tennessee

If you think that I left home for only the second time in my life, along with my fiancée, family and friends without being a little afraid you are right! Visions of "Deliverance" came to mind. I had this mental image of me being the only "normal" person driving a Ford with everyone else driving Dodges and Chevrolets (God forbid). My history with the South had not been much of a happy one. First there was the military, and then there was my escaping there with full intentions of dying. I did not see myself having a happy time in Tennessee. I did not exactly drool at the thought of leaving my loved ones behind and going South.

Let me tell you something about traffic in the South. They have none. We complain about getting tickets for driving five miles per hour over the speed limit. Forget that. In the south, you have to be driving fifteen over *and* be drinking the wrong kind of drink (Coors) or throwing bottles out the window at a passing policeman. Then they *might* pull you over to see if something was wrong, like ask if you had broken up with your wife-mother-daughter-cousin or punched out your father-uncle-brother. Or broken up with your dog.

I love driving in the South. The Ford hummed. The further South I went, the fewer hot rods I saw. I guess I had this mental image of seeing lots of cars and trucks up on blocks but I saw none. Vehicles in the South were better kept than in the North because they did not use salt on the roads. My truck was the anomaly, *I* was the red neck driving a souped up truck. People pulled over when they saw me coming up behind them on back roads. No joke, they pulled over. I usually was going faster than other traffic and so people would just pull over and wave me by. We would never think of doing that in the North.

They hated my truck in town. There were parking lines in front of the apartment but I received a total of five tickets. They would write things like, "parked outside of lines", "obstructing sidewalk", "obstructing a thoroughfare". I really think the police in town just hated my truck. Of course I did give them reason. People there drove in a leisurely fashion with no hurry. I was always in a hurry. I would pass people up left and right. I did not get speeding tickets, only parking tickets.

At the factory, *I* was that damned Yankee! I made friends though. People there were open hearted and generous. I enjoyed the people I worked with. You hear about drive by shootings in cities in the north, west and Florida? A drive by shooting in Tennessee usually involves a deer and a thirty ought six rifle sticking out the window! In Ohio, if someone waves at you, it usually is the middle finger. In the South, the police waved at you and they were just saying "howdy" as they drove by you. The first time a policeman waved at me, I pulled over. I thought he was getting me for something. Like driving a Ford. But he was just waving hi.

People talk in Tennessee. Across the road from my apartment there was a small grocery story. The men would sit on the front porch and just talk.

One day an older gentleman saw me with my .22 and came over and asked if he could see it. He fell in love with it because he recognized it for what it was. He offered me four hundred dollars for it on the spot. I told him no, that my grandfather had given it to me.

I had one complaint. The music. I love music, but country is not music. Country music is an oxymoron and country music awards are a double oxymoron. The only music station in the area played country. The only music they sold in town...was country. I fortunately had a selection of music with me to listen to that did not involve banjoes or violins played a certain way. Taking violins out of classical music and playing them...*that* way is just a sin folks!

Lexington, Tennessee is a small burg in the center of nowhere. If you look between Nashville and Memphis, there is a dot that says Jackson. Jackson is five times larger than Lexington which is thirty five miles from Jackson. However, it has two redeeming draws. The houses and the lakes. Houses which would be one million dollars in the North are two hundred thousand. And there are large lakes everywhere. Wal-Mart is the center of social life. I saw a family one day who were all dressed in black and white square outfits. I think they used the tablecloth and made their clothes.

At work, I was on an assembly line, putting together hinge pieces for Ford trucks and cars. However, after a few weeks, they saw that I had computer experience on my application and asked if I would like to run the miller welder. The miller welder was a beast. It supplied the entire line with parts. It is a giant steel wheel laying flat and is about ten feet across with twelve positions around it that it stops at as it turns. One of the positions was for me to put the main part on. Some of the other positions also automatically fed parts, then there were welding guns which would drop down on other positions and weld the parts onto the part I placed on it in the first place.

All I had to do was put my one part on and make certain the welders ran right and refill the other part feeders. Something went wrong every five minutes with the blasted godless beast. Welding tips would build up slag I had to wash off. Parts would jam in the part placers. Too much weld would go on a part. Not enough weld would go on a part. If it got behind, the whole line of workers got behind and stood there looking at you wondering why they weren't working. But it was the most important position on the line and I lived with it.

What I could not live with was management telling us five minutes to quitting time that we had to work another three hours. We were supposed to work eight hours. *Supposed* to. They would wait until five minutes before quitting time over and over then tell us we had to work three or four more hours. Why? Because in Tennessee, there are no unions and they can do it. I would kick the crap out of parts boxes (large metal tubs) when they would do this. I could not control my anger but I didn't break anything so nobody said anything. It was almost expected. They would tell us to stay another three hours and my team mates would look at me to see what I would do. That was sad.

At the end of February, Mai and I announced to our individual families that we were getting married. Now, in the Vietnamese custom, it is the man who takes care of all the preparations for the wedding. All of it. I spent an incredible amount of time calling Dayton talking to rental halls, clothing stores, photographers, alcohol carriers, etc. During breaks at work (two day weekends occasionally or more) I would drive up to Dayton and take care of things. John and his brother would be my best men. Hoa and Mai's friend, Nga would be the bridesmaids.

We wanted to get married in June or July but finally had to settle on August twenty seventh. Up until the first week of August, managers and people at work thought we would be living in Tennessee, but then I put in my two week notice. I had wanted to honeymoon at Estes' Park, in Colorado and had tickets already set to be picked up at the airport and reservations made at the Holidome in Estes. Then Mai told me that flying or long drives made her sick. Scratch Colorado. So I made arrangements for our honeymoon to be in Hocking Hills, Ohio. The week before the wedding, I moved all of my stuff back up to Ohio and stayed at my parents for the week.

Chapter Thirteen
Marriage and Career: Dealing with Bipolar

I learned something about Vietnamese weddings. People do not give presents at the wedding. They give cash. We more than made back what I had spent on arranging the wedding. We also received a 1987 Thunderbird from Mai's sister, Khuyen. Mai changed clothes at the reception four times. It is a big thing for a Vietnamese bride to change clothes several times during the reception, each time to a different type of dress. The reception went on for hours. It was around midnight when we finally got out and went to a local hotel to sleep before going on our honeymoon the next day.

When we returned from the honeymoon, I sent out several dozen resumes. One of the first ones I received a call back from was Electronic Data Systems, Ross Perot's old company. I took the position and would work there from November, 1994 until October, 1996. I was an output operator, printing out huge print jobs from the mainframe. I also output jobs to tape operations, reel to reel and microfiche. On weekends I would often help swap out old mainframes for new ones, or pull bus and tag lines and lay down fiber optic lines instead.

In 1995, I wanted something else to drive instead of my truck. I was tired of the noise from the loud exhaust (so were our apartment neighbors, I am quite sure), and I was tired of the low gas mileage. I had wrecked the eighty seven thunderbird and wanted another car. I drove to

Maranatha auto dealers in the truck and saw a Porsche. The guy came out and asked, "You interested in that Porsche?" I told him I was. He asked me what kind of driving I liked and I told him what I looked for in a car. He told me I did not want the Porsche but wanted the 1985 Volvo he had for the same price as the Porsche. I test drove it and he was right! The Volvo was powerful and handled wonderfully. I would put over two hundred thousand miles on that car before I would donate it to the Mission in 2006.

At EDS, I was in an intensive training program called the OPD program. This consisted of thirteen onsite exams and five offsite exams at world headquarters in Plano, Texas. If you flunked three exams, you were out of the company. I flunked three times. Unlike college, where I was in my element and enjoyed what I was doing, studying the books at EDS was "*work*". Most of the books were teaching me programming languages to pull jobs off a mainframe. My mind could not wrap itself around the books and pay attention.

On November twenty nine, 1995, Jordan Peter Young was born at Kettering Hospital. Mai's water broke at eleven o'clock pm and the first thought in my head was, "I don't have to go to work tomorrow!" I named him Jordan after my grandmother McAllister's maiden name and Peter for Mai's Catholic side. You see, I am a Scot/Irish Calvinist, married to a Vietnamese Catholic! Mai was in labor for twenty three hours. Just after delivery, Mother stayed with Mai while Father and I drove back to Mai's and my apartment so I could change clothes. On the way back to the hospital I was speeding and we got pulled over. As soon as the policeman walked up, I told the policeman my wife just gave birth and he told me to take off.

After leaving EDS, I was offered a job with National Cash Register (NCR) in Dayton. There, I was doing service invoicing, invoicing customers for work done on their ATM machines. I made a number of friends and did not seem to have any problems with my bipolar the first two years at work, but I had many anger issues going on at home. I also developed a lasting love for photography and bought a Canon SLR with a 28-300 zoom lens. Later, a few companies would hire me to take pics of various functions they were having. It was during this time also, that I did the senior pictures for Temple Christian School.

One of Mai's close friends at the time at Morning Pride was a Korean lady named Hee Markley. Hee's husband is American and they both attended a Korean Assembly of God in Beavercreek quite close to our apartment. Hee invited us to come to her church and we went once. Mai did not go back after that but I did, liking the services. The pastor preached in Korean, but his son in a soundproof room interpreted it into English and we American men wore headphones so we could hear the sermon in English. Very cool! Plus, afterwards, the women had huge amounts of Korean food including kimchi which I love.

Pastor Park knew what my background was and asked me to teach the children in Bible class. He told me they had nobody to do it. I accepted his offer and would end up teaching them for the next year and a half. The age range was from twelve years old up to fourteen years. We would take the kids on outings, including Ohio Caverns. I stopped teaching when less and less children showed up because their parents were leaving the church to go to a larger Korean church in Kettering.

Mai and I wanted a house. Harold and Khuyen owned the house in Riverside where the family lived. They offered us that house for considerably less than it was worth if we would let the family keep living there. At that time it was four of the sisters living there, Mai's mother and her niece and nephew. One of the sisters got married and moved out and we moved into the house in 1996, with ten people living there in total including the four of us. I think it was during this time that my hair truly started turning gray!

January eleventh, 1998, Tristan John Young was born at Miami Valley Hospital. I named him Tristan after the character Brad Pitt played on "Legends of the Fall" and John for the Catholic side. Jordan takes after my side of the family. At age fifteen, Jordan stands six feet two inches tall while Tristan, at age thirteen and four feet ten inches tall, takes after his mother's side of the family. Emotionally though they are switched. Jordan takes after Mai in that both hide their emotions deeply. Tristan and I wear our emotions outside where everyone can see them. Both of us are huggers while Jordan and Mai are not.

In November, 1998, a Thai friend of Mai's named Pada got me on in the Order Realization Center (ORC) at NCR which was on the other side of World Head Quarters. There were a number of Asians at NCR and I was invited to join the NCR 4A which consisted of Asians, Arabs and other non-white minorities. I was the only American in the club and was VP in charge of elections. When election time came around each year, I would send out ballots to all those in the club so they could vote on who they wanted to fill the various positions in the club. One of my friends at work gave me the nickname of Saigon Surfer because I liked surfing so much and because my wife is from Saigon.

In September, 1999, the entire family moved to Kettering, leaving the four of us with the house in Riverside. The house by the way has an indoor, in-ground two thousand gallon swimming pool. Because a pump and heater were not hooked up, I roofed it over and turned it into a Dungeons and Dragon room. Later, I would tear the roof back off of it and we just used it for storage. We did have it filled with water once in the summertime, but even with the glass walls around three sides of it, it was still too cold to use.

Bipolar disease can cause manic episodes to occur. These can manifest as rage or feelings of extremely heightened emotion or purpose. During my college days, I rode these highs to get straight A's in school. Now I turned that same heightened emotion to building a giant tree house behind our house in a large locust tree. In the middle of summer, I put together a large tree house which would sleep four to six adults comfortably. I also designed a chess board out of wood and ceramic tiles which compared to the best of any I had ever seen. Jordan taught me how to play chess but Tristan and I were the ones who would often play. Tristan beats me almost every time we play! I started taking him to the Dayton Chess club where he also wowed people there with his skills. Later at Paxar, a couple of the managers would routinely play me at chess. The tree house would stay up for about three years until I tore it down because it had turned into a spider trap! Spider webs covered the inside of it and since I am arachnophobic, I wanted nothing to do with them.

At the end of December, 1999, NCR laid off a huge amount of us. I went from NCR to Paxar's Graphic's Division in Huber Heights, Ohio. There, I would input orders for printed jobs and then go out to the plant and schmooze the operators to try and get rush jobs out sooner than normal. At Paxar, I met Craig, a fellow Christian who to this day has remained my best friend. I saw Craig go through a divorce and he left his nice house and went to live in a trailer. One month later it was Halloween. I rented a batman outfit to wear at work for the Halloween party. The outfit had twelve pieces and I needed help putting the thing on so I asked Craig to help me. We were in the men's locker room and he was helping me squeeze into the parts and suddenly he stopped and said to me, "a month ago, I was married to a beautiful woman, living in a beautiful house with three children who loved me and now I am divorced, living in a trailer home, broke and helping batman put on his clothes!"

My 1985 Volvo was nearing the end of its life. I had put two hundred thousand miles on it and it was coming down with a terminal case of body cancer. I bought a 1998 Volvo S90. Mai had a 1998 Toyota Camry XLE. I stopped driving the 1985 Volvo.

My niece, Ashley and I were becoming close. I thought of her as a daughter. She was about fourteen at this time and I was her ride when she needed to go somewhere. I took her to the doctor and dentist. I took her to movies and shopping. I had fun with her and looked forward to the little hugs I got from her. One day, she, myself and her friend Timmy (a girl), saw a movie at the local theatre. Afterwards we couldn't find my car. With me in the lead and them back behind me running, we ran through the parking lot at Dayton Mall looking for my car. Then the humor of the situation caught me. I imagined what it looked like to people to see two young pretty girls chasing a middle aged man in a crowded parking lot. I had to stop and laugh and we all three laughed over it. Later, when Ashley turned sixteen, I let her drive my new Volvo when she had her temps and she asked me what would happen if she wrecked it. I looked at her and told her, "That's what insurance is for!"

During this time period, I bought a new toy to play with, ordered from California. I bought it after seeing some surfers riding one on television and gave into my impetuousness. It is called a "Carveboard". It looks like a large skateboard with large inflatable tires. It rides like a surfboard on land. The entire board tilts on its axis, so to turn I simply lean over to the right or left and the entire board turns in that direction. If I went around a turn fast enough, my entire body would be perpendicular to the ground and I could read out my hand and ride it on the ground, like riding a wave. When I first started riding it at the local skate parks, I became a sensation. People would stop and watch and sometimes take pictures. I had three accidents on it but nothing dampened my enjoyment of surfing the pavement on the board.

I love Lemans style auto racing. I love Eurocars. Two hours away, North of Columbus is Mid-Ohio Lemans. I bought a ticket and drove my '98 Volvo there. I flew through the back country roads and coming over a hill, had to put on my breaks hard. There was a black buggy with horses pulling it. I just about mowed down the Amish person driving the buggy! That day, I saw several more such buggies in the same area. The race was awesome, with Porsches wiping out in one race and a Ferrari flipping into the air in another. Some of the drivers were still in their teens. I had paid extra for the paddock pass which allowed me to go down into the infield where the drivers were tuning their cars so I could take pictures. It also allowed me to park infield where staff and drivers were parked rather than outside where everyone else parked. On top of special parking, I was in a stand reserved for paddock pass parking only, which was just outside of an "S curve" so I could see numerous wipeouts.

At Paxar, my bipolar was affecting me like never before in my life. I was going up and down within seconds at home, being enraged one second and dangerously depressed the next. Sometimes I felt like I was going mad with my life riding the two extremes of depression and mania. At work, I would pace while talking on the phone to customers then hang up and slam the phone against the wall if I were having problems with a client. I was wildly out of control. I had been to the doctor who put me on Ritalin and Stratera, but neither one did anything for me. I wasn't on either medicine long enough to find out if they would work anyhow. Then in June of 2005, I made a ten thousand dollar error because I wasn't paying attention. As usual, I was going too fast on something and did not notice an error and hit enter. Again, I was out of a job due to my bipolar disease and ADHD.

Chapter Fourteen
Suicide Attempts and Second College

Losing my job at Paxar was a blow I could not take. I was already being buffeted by the winds of my depression and rage. Then, on top of the layoff and not finding another job and Mai's sadness over it all, came Hurricane Katrina to Louisiana. I saw how our government did nothing for the people there and that was the tipping point. When Mai was at work and the boys were in school, I turned on both Volvos in the garage and put towels along the cracks of the garage door and sat in the 1998 Volvo writing my suicide note. But two hours later, I felt no ill effects from the exhaust fumes and realized I wouldn't die this way. That night I told Mai what I had done and she told me I needed to get help.

With 2006 coming on, we talked and decided I would go back to school and get a second degree, this time in the medical field as a medical assistant. We picked the National College of Business just because it had higher ratings online than most of the fly by night colleges. I spent two years at the National College of Business, going full-time. I was on the Dean's list and Honor roll as usual and ate up my classes. This time, the mathematics clicked on as though a switch in my brain had turned on. I knew I was making an impact on those around me when we went into a class at the beginning of a new quarter and two kids sat on either side of me and one of the kids coming through the door groaned. The professor asked him what was wrong and he said, "I wanted to sit beside Kevin because he always makes A's!"

I went to work for Echoing Valley Residential Care Facility in January, 2006. There were thirty six MRDD (mentally retarded, developmentally disabled) residents who lived there and I helped take care of the men. Everything from brushing their teeth to wiping them after they used the bathroom. Things I once said I would never do I learned to appreciate as I made friends with the residents who lived there. Some of them could do nothing except move their eyes and make a few sounds, but they could communicate volumes with just their eyes. Unfortunately, there was one autistic boy there who was large and stole drinks from all of us as well as the residents. My continued impatience with this caused me to scream at him one day and I was gone, yet again a victim to my bipolarity after only being with Echoing Valley thirteen months.

I graduated from National College just a few months before I lost my job at Echoing Valley. This time, my depression lasted for weeks. I was at the bottom in a deep trough from which I could see no light. There was no sunlight in my life, nothing that caused me joy. I stayed in bed sometimes eighteen hours a day, hoping for death. After several weeks of this I gave up completely. I blew up at Mai one night over something stupid and immediately stormed out into the garage where I had my new suicide method waiting. I drove my 1998 Volvo to a local hotel. I picked up the plastic capsule I had and opened it and poured out its contents; a large pellet of mercury. I put it in my mouth and swallowed it and drank a coke and waited to die while listening to "Bittersweet Symphony" by *The Verve.* My own little mercury cocktail.

Do you know that mercury is the second most deadly toxin in the world behind radiation poisoning? I sat for an hour and a half waiting to go into the convulsions I figured would go with the large amount I had taken. I wanted to die completely in every way. Nothing happened. I drove home.

At home Mai was already in bed. I researched mercury more and found out that the human body will not digest mercury in its natural state. In fact, around one hundred years ago, mercury was taken as a laxative for constipation for children. I couldn't even kill myself.

Mai put up with all of these things patiently. If I believed in "sainthood", she would be one. She has never said a bad word to me nor ever done a bad thing that I have ever seen. There is no such thing as a perfect person but she is close. As the years have gone by, my love for her has only grown.

In March, 2007, I started working for a home healthcare agency called Rescare. I had a load of clients whom I took care of in their houses. One particular woman I took care of more than anyone was in Beavercreek, close to our house. As time went by, my time with her became more and my time with other clients lessened. About one year after I started taking care of her, she developed pneumonia while in the hospital for some tests and passed away. Her son hired me privately to take care of his father at the same address. I continue to do this to this day, plus take care of clients under Rescare on a part-time basis.

In March, 2008, I started working for Primed Cardiology in Kettering. I worked for one doctor who was in a group of five cardiologists at the same building. My duties included triaging patients, taking vitals, giving shots, drawing blood, keeping up the charts and scheduling patients for procedures and surgeries in the office, hospital and at other facilities. The patients loved me and sometimes brought me in gifts, but I had one terrible problem with paying attention to the charts because my mind would race so fast that I would miss things. The doctor started getting on me about this and eventually, in February of 2009, I would lose my job.

Chapter Fifteen
Bipolar Diagnosis with ADHD: The Beginning of Healing

In July, 2009, my doctor said she believed me to be Bipolar 1 with rapid cycling phases along with ADHD. I had never thought of the possibility of me being bipolar and did not even want to consider it due to the stigma I had about mental diseases. To me, someone who had bipolar disease was nuts! I ignored the doctor's idea and did not go on any medications.

In June, 2009, I went to work for Workflow One in Dayton, working customer service for clients. I also entered orders into the system for customers. In January of 2010, I was losing control again and the depression and anger swings were going back to being a daily thing. I was heavily into Facebook at this time and making friends that I hadn't seen in decades. On January fifteenth, I accepted the fact that I was bipolar from reading on the Internet about the symptoms. I called my niece and told her I was bipolar and she accepted it easily, telling me she had figured my problem was something like that. That was the stimulus I needed. I broke down crying, as being accepted for how I was by one of the main people in my life was what I needed. It made me accept myself also. I went to the doctor a couple of days later and broke down crying, telling the doctor I accepted her diagnosis of bipolar 1 with rapid cycling and to please put me on medication. She started me out on a low dose of Depakote, with the idea being to increase it as time went by. I made friends on Facebook with Anthea Whitwell, a fellow bipolar living in Australia and we had many talks about how both of us felt when under the effects of the disease. We also shared a kindred interest in writing.

As time went by, I became so comfortable with what I was doing at work that I would sometimes forget to check my work before hitting the enter button. On one such occasion, I hit the enter button without noticing I had double keyed a number in and again, it caused a ten thousand dollar order instead of a five thousand dollar order. I was let go from Workflow One on February eleventh, 2010. The depression I felt was the same as in March, 2007 and I became deeply suicidal again. The night I was fired, I emailed Anthea and told her I might kill myself that night. I also emailed my niece and told her the same thing. Ashley called me, crying and told me if I felt like killing myself to go to the hospital. Anthea emailed me, saying the same thing. After much talk with both of them, I swore to both that I would go to the hospital if I felt like killing myself.

I realized that night that as lonely in Bipolar as I felt, I had to stop bringing my loved ones into it the way I had done to my niece. I needed people I could go to who would understand what I was feeling and who I could bounce my emotions off of without affecting them. Anthea was my bouncing board, plus I went to a counseling session with "High Flyers, Low Landers" at Miami Valley Hospital.

The next week, I went back to the doctor and told her what had happened, breaking down crying in the process of telling her. She increased my Depakote to two thousand milligrams daily. I would be out of work, apart from the gentleman I take care of privately from February eleventh, 2010 until January of 2011. The Depakote evened out my depression and manic rage swings and I also was started on Strattera, Cogentin and Saphris. By February, 2011, the mood swings are almost completely gone except for some minor impatience I still get with things that come along outside my normal schedule. I do not have the deep depressions any more, nor do I have the rages except extremely rarely. I am hopeful for the future at this point. I also started reading everything I could get my hands on about bipolar disease, including one interesting book called "Touched With Fire" by Kay Redfield Jamison. In it, she expostulated the idea that the high manic episodes in Bipolar were what made some people become artists and writers. She also hypothesized that people who took mood stabilizers lost their ability to think creatively. I myself can attest to that, because once I was well into taking two thousand milligrams a day of Depakote, my creativity disappeared as far as poetry is concerned.

Watching the extreme emotional depths disappear has not happened overnight when I started taking the medicine. It took six months before the medicines were to the point where I no longer saw deadly depressions or daily rages. Bipolarity is a disease of steps. Step ups in the medicine or steps to other medicines because the others did not work. It really shouldn't be called a mental disease, as it is rather a chemical imbalance within the body. It is like diabetes in that one doesn't get it for doing something to themselves like alcohol or drugs but because of chemicals imbalanced in the anatomy. A movement is on in Congress in fact to have it removed from being a mental disease and have it relabeled as a chemical imbalance.

I have felt like "damaged goods" for most of my life. I have the skills to succeed at life but being bipolar has put a bad wrapping on it. As the medicine evens out my emotions more, I can hope that I can get to the point where not only will nobody else notice the bipolarity in me, but I myself will not notice it. Because I have failed my way through life except for college, I rigidly push our boys to excel in school. Mai and the boys know when I get angry occasionally for some stupid reason or other, that it is the bipolar doing it.

I feel things on an emotional level that others without bipolar simply cannot understand. To be bipolar is to feel EVERYTHING to its depths or its highest. Every depression is THE depression. To be happy is THE happiest moment. I cry at the tear jerker movies. Certain songs have brought tears to me. When someone else is sad, I feel their sadness. If they are happy, I am happy with them and want the best for them. Patients in the cardiology room who would cry would get hugs from me and find me crying for them. Being bipolar is not all bad in that it gives us an insight into others' emotions and an ability to experience the world at depths and heights others can never see or feel. It is to touch the fire up there and the bottom of the river down there.

In June, 2010, at the urging of Anthea, I had all my poetry published in a book composed of all fifty one of my poems. The book is called, 'Shadows in a Mad World", published by Chipmunkapublishing. In February of 2011, I once again started taking care of clients through Rescare Health Care along with the gentleman I take care of privately. I am also working on two other books, a novel length western and a Christian science fiction novel. The creativity has dulled though because I am on the mood stabilizers which prohibit my creativity from coming through the way it did before I started taking the medicines. I can live with this though over the alternative! I see only a bright light at the end of the tunnel now since my dark days seem to be over for the most part.

If there is one bad thing about the mood stabilizers it is one of the side effects; shakiness of my hands and head. Sometimes I can hide it but other times it is quite noticeable to others, especially the shakiness in my hands. I look like a palsied old man when my hands really get going! This side effect though, again, is bearable considering the alternative.

I have never been an alcoholic or a drug user. I did try marijuana once in my twenties but it was not something I ever wanted to do again since. The alcohol I drink is rare, maybe four times a year if that and then it is either Absinthe, Long Island Ice Teas, or Cognac. I despise beer, wine and champagne and could live without alcohol probably for the rest of my life. Iced tea and milk are my drinks of choice, especially real milk with all the cream still in it. Smoking was something I also did in my twenties, especially the pipe, but it has all gone by the wayside.

Living on this side of the killer depressions and "Wrath of God rages" all looks brighter. I still have days when I am impatient with others but they are rare. I still have very rare days where I feel melancholy, but I have so much to live for now. Our boys will soon be off to college within the next four years and I have grandchildren to look forward to as well as weddings not only of our boys, but my nephew and nieces. I would like to walk my niece, Ashley Hoang down the aisle one day as she was closest to being like my daughter since her father died when she was three or so. I smile more now and am content. It is an ever ongoing thing with the medicines to get them just right but I know I am on the right path.

www.ingramcontent.com/pod-product-compliance
Lightning Source LLC
Chambersburg PA
CBHW031220290326
41931CB00035B/620